SAME HOUSE, DIFFERENT HOMES

Why Adult Children of Alcoholics Are Not All the Same

Robert J. Ackerman, Ph.D.
Indiana University of Pennsylvania

Robert J. Ackerman, Ph.D.
Indiana University of Pennsylvania
Indiana, Pennsylvania

Library of Congress Cataloging-in-Publication Data

Filed

© 1987   Health Communications, Inc.
1721 Blount Road
Pompano Beach, Florida 33069

ISBN 0-932194-43-5

Cover design by Reta Kaufman

ACKNOWLEDGMENTS

I would like to thank the more than one thousand adults who participated in the study upon which much of this book is based. Your willingness to share yourself is greatly appreciated. A special thank you is due Joyce Tang for her assistance in processing the questionnaires and to Georgia Springer for her adminstrative support. I am especially indebted to Judy Michaels, as my research assistant on this project, and for her endless hours of support and hard work. Her contributions to this booklet are enormous.

To Oliver Ford, for his editorial expertise and ideas I owe a special thank you. His support of my work and his encouragement are deeply appreciated. Finally, I want to acknowledge the support of the Graduate School and the Faculty Research Associate Program of Indiana University of Pennsylvania without which this project would not have been possible.

DEDICATION

for
Kimberly, Jason and Robert

CONTENTS

TABLES

Section One

Understanding Differences Among Adult Children of Alcoholics

An "adult child" of an alcoholic is any adult who, as a child, was reared by one or two alcoholic parents. In the United States today there are twenty two million people who fit this definition.

Much of the current attention to adult children of alcoholics is largely the result of the concern in the past ten years for young children of alcoholics. When the children of alcoholics movement began approximately ten years ago, there was very little attention being paid to young children of alcoholics, and adult children of alcoholics were not even recognized. Today it is the adult children of alcoholics who dominate the movement, for which there may be several causes.

There are more than three times as many adult children of alcoholics as there are adolescent and young children of alcoholics.

Many of the people working on behalf of young children of alcoholics are themselves adult children and thus working with young children raises many of the same issues in them.

When adult children were young, there were no children of alcoholics programs for them so an entire generation of adult children of alcoholics has emerged on the scene all at once and all in search of understanding, intervention or support for their childhood experiences.

To understand these experiences and adult children of alcoholics better, a National Adult Children of Alcoholics Research Study was undertaken (Ackerman, 1987). Much of the information in this book is based on the findings of this study, which utilized the responses of approximately one thousand adults. Of these, approximately five hundred were adult children of alcoholics, and five hundred were adults raised by non-alcoholic parents (see Appendix for further information about the study). Some of the goals of this study were to examine not only the effects of exposure to parental alcoholism, but also to examine what may have contributed to differences among adult children of alcoholics.

Although adult children of alcoholics may share many similar experiences from having grown up in an alcoholic family, they are not all affected in the same way. One adult child may be devastated by the parental alcoholism, another becomes withdrawn and isolated, and another survives well and emerges with few problems. Sometimes only one of the children in a family will accept or acknowledge the alcoholism, whereas others continue to deny not only the alcoholism but also that they were affected at all.

It is perhaps ironic that I have met so many adult children of alcoholics whose brothers and sisters are not adult children of alcoholics! To understand these differences among adult children of alcoholics, one needs to consider the intervening variables in their experiences as the child of an alcoholic. Some of these variables may include the degree of alcoholism experienced, the type and kind of alcoholic in the family, the child's perception of the experience, the child's resilience to stress, the gender of the alcoholic and the child, the age at which the adult child was exposed to alcoholism, any positive offsetting factors while growing up, and any cultural considerations and implications. The different effects of these variables are not limited to childhood, but later will manifest themselves in a variety of ways in the adult.

Obviously, many of the concerns and behaviors of adult children today were caused by their experiences in childhood. Therefore, the following variables are discussed not only as they may have affected the adult child of an alcoholic while he or she was growing up, but also as they may be affecting him or her today.

If you are an adult child, you may recognize aspects of your own experience and personality, not only in the responses of Adult Children of Alcoholics but also in those of the children of non-alcoholic parents. From this you can begin to understand better who you are and are not, how that came to be, and that it doesn't have to stay that way. Even better, you may come to understand and accept yourself, more secure in the knowledge that increasingly your responses will be indistinguishable from those of the children of non-alcoholic parents.

(4) SAME HOUSE, DIFFERENT HOMES

Section Two

The Degree of Alcoholism and Its Effects on Parenting

Consideration of the degree of alcoholism found in the alcoholic assesses how significantly the alcoholism affected the ability of the parent while the child was growing up. Although a parent may be alcoholic, he or she is first and foremost a parent to the child. How the alcoholic adult fulfills his or her role as a parent affects children more than the drinking does. After all, if the drinking were not leading to dysfunctional behaviors, no one would be upset with the drinking. It is the inability of the alcoholic parent to fulfill his or her various parental roles successfully that becomes detrimental to these children around the alcoholic.

All adults occupy several roles simultaneously, but most adults identify with a particular role that they fulfill more than other roles. This role can be called the "master status" role. Additionally, others can see the adult from a particular role that is important to the observer.

For children, the adult caretaker in their lives occupies the master status role of parent. If the adult next door is an alcoholic, that is very different from your own parent being alcoholic, because the adult next door does not occupy the same master status for you. Thus, for the child growing up, the question resulting from parental alcoholism is: how does this alcoholism affect the quality of child care?

For example, many alcoholics may be able to function outside of their family and to maintain friends, jobs, et cetera, but not be able to function appropriately as a parent. In fact, it would not be uncommon for some adult children to remember and resent that the alcoholic parent was nice to everyone but his or her own family.

Other adult children may feel that the parent tried to parent effectively, but was not able to meet the emotional needs of the children. The role impairment caused by alcoholism that is most significant for children of alcoholics obviously is the impairment of the alcoholic as their parent.

Section Three

What Type or Kind of Alcoholic Parent Did the Adult Child Have?

Not all alcoholic parents act the same, nor fulfill their parental roles the same. To assess the different impacts on adult children, one should examine the different behavioral and parenting styles of the alcoholic parents.

The expression, *type of alcoholic*, refers to the personality type, whereas *kind of alcoholic* refers to the kinds of behavior that the alcoholic parent engaged in, particularly when he or she was drinking. Although one could argue that personality and behavior are the same, for the sake of argument let's look at them separately.

Young children seem to be able to do this. The child may say, "I can't stand it when my mother is drinking" or "I hate it when my dad is drunk," but that does not mean that the child can't stand mother or hates dad. The child is able to separate the person from the behavior. Also in many alcoholic families, family members distinguish between alcohol behavior and sober behavior by such statements as "he (or she) is the greatest person when he (or she) is sober, but watch out for him (her) when he (she) is drinking." It is as if they understand that, under the influence of alcohol, the parent undergoes a personality change.

These changes may have increased the problems in childhood for adult children because of the amount and variety of role inconsistency in the alcoholic parent to whom they were exposed.

In Table 1 the different types of behaviors in the alcoholic parent are identified, along with the prevalence of each noted by adult children of alcoholics. This table not only illustrates the differences in behaviors found among alcoholics when drinking, but also that the adult children identified more than one behavior occurring in the same alcoholic. These different behaviors within the same individual further confuse the inconsistent role playing already being experienced in the family.

TABLE 1
Alcoholic's Behavior When Drinking as Identified by Adult Children of Alcoholics

Type of Behavior*	Identified in Alcoholic Parent (Percentage of Yes Responses)
Verbally Belligerent	49.0%
Offensive	41.5
Passive	31.0
Carefree	13.5
Other	14.3

*More than one behavior could be identified

As indicated in the above table, verbal belligerence was the most common form of behavior identified by adult children in their alcoholic parents. This was followed by offensive behavior, which could have ranged from embarrassment to abuse. The next most commonly identified behavior was passivity in the alcoholic, followed by being carefree and by other forms of behavior. It is obvious that not only does alcoholism profoundly affect life for the child, but also the forms of behaviors associated with the alcoholic in and of themselves may be extremely difficult to tolerate. Thus the adult child may have learned to adapt to alcoholism and to highly undesirable behaviors in a parent simultaneously.

TABLE 2
Behavior of Alcoholic Parents and the Degree of Effect on the Lives of Adult Children of Alcoholics

Alcoholic's Behavior When Drinking	Degree of Effect		
	Low	Moderate	High
Offensive	3.8%	7.7%	88.5%
Verbally Belligerent	6.5	9.3	84.2
Passive	12.2	12.2	75.6
Carefree	22.1	4.4	73.5
Other	20.8	9.7	69.5

Do some of these behaviors combined with alcoholism affect adult children differently and thus increase or lessen the impact of parental alcoholism? In Table 2 the different types of behaviors found in alcoholic parents are compared as to how significantly the adult children felt they were affected by the alcoholism (see Table 2). The table shows that not only were the majority of adult children highly affected by the alcoholism, but also that the type of behavior displayed by the alcoholic parent contributed to how significantly they felt that they were affected.

Alcoholism coupled with offensive behavior was found to affect adult children the most, even though as indicated on Table 1, verbal belligerence was the most commonly associated behavior. The next highest effect was found among adult children with verbally belligerent alcoholic parents, followed by passive, carefree, and other types of behaviors.

The key to surviving an alcoholic family is the ability to adapt to the situation. Sharon Wegscheider-Cruse states, "the ability to survive nonsense requires manipulation" (Wegscheider-Cruse, 1978). In the alcoholic family this manipulation occurs at two levels at least. First, the alcoholic learns to manipulate everyone else, so that he or she can deny and continue the drinking. After awhile the non-alcoholic family members will then begin to manipulate themselves so as not to "rock the boat," thus establishing a second level of manipulation. The adult child may be able to remember many times when he or she was quiet, kept things to himself or herself, or made sure that the alcoholic did not have access to information. Thus, depending on the mood or behavior of the alcoholic parent, the child responded in a particular way, but perhaps inconsistently.

For example, the alcoholic parent engages in a lot of inconsistent role behavior by fulfilling his or her roles in at least four ways. He or she plays one role when sober, and another when drunk. A third role is played when the alcoholic becomes highly anxious or agitated, which is usually before drinking. The fourth way occurs when the alcoholic is having a hangover and/or feels guilty or remorseful. A typical scenario could be that on Friday night and Saturday, all hell is breaking loose. Sunday is hangover day, and Monday is full of guilt and remorse. Tuesday and Wednesday are fairly calm. Thursday begins with anxiety and agitation, which leads to drinking on Friday, and the cycle begins again.

Just imagine yourself as a child in this family who wants to ask for something. Like most children you hope to get what you want. What day of the week would you ask? Some may ask on Tuesday or Wednesday because this would appear to be the most normal time to ask. However, many adult children remember asking on particular days when they felt that the probability of compliance was the greatest. Therefore, some would pick hangover or guilt days, whereas others would ask when the alcoholic was drinking.

I remember a woman in New York stating to me "I always asked my father when he was drunk because then he would give me whatever I wanted." After a while, the adult child learned that the probability of the pay-off was more important than the health of the request. However, the adult child may remember that he or she also felt guilty or remorseful, because he or she had used the guilt or remorse of the alcoholic to get what he or she wanted. Furthermore, the adult child may have felt angry or resentful that he or she had to "manipulate" the situation to get what he or she wanted, rather than being able to ask any day of the week. Thus the child also is drawn into

the manipulation game and experiences inconsistency personally, as well as on the parental level.

This manipulation of each other becomes evident when one
looks at other issues associated with the type or kind of alcoholic that the adult child experienced. Alcoholic parents who
were extremely passive and spent much of their time sleeping
or drinking away from home may have affected their child one
way. Alcoholics who were extremely belligerent verbally may
have affected their child in entirely different ways.

Another type of alcoholic parent is the parent who treats
everything in life as a joke; all the alcoholic does is to make
light of everything and to accuse everyone of being too serious.
This could have been stressful for the adult child while growing up because he or she never could count on the alcoholic
for serious responses, support or adequate parental advice.

Additionally, there is the alcoholic parent who became ag-
gressive and engaged in family violence, and thus the adult
child was in the position of "double-jeopardy." Not only did
adult children with an abusive parent experience parental alcoholism, but also they were subjected to child abuse, sexual
abuse, or to witnessing spouse abuse.

Parents who were binge drinkers may have had different
effects on the adult child than parents who depended upon
daily intake of alcohol. There are also parents who although
alcoholic, did not bring out extreme negative feelings in their
children, because the adult child perceived that he or she was
still loved in spite of the alcoholism.

Just as different parenting styles affect children differently,
so do different types of alcoholics and their behaviors or per-
sonalities affect their children differently. The adult child may
remember that when the parent was drunk, he or she acted a
certain way, but when the parent was sober, he or she could be
more himself/herself. When the alcoholic parent was agitated,
however, the adult child may remember being very careful to
stay well out of their way.

I once heard Jael Greenleaf address an audience of adult
children of alcoholics in Los Angeles and say that she believed
that most adult children considered themselves to be clair-

voyant (Greenleaf, 1984). I remember thinking to myself, "That isn't true, but I knew you were going to say that." It may not be clairvoyance, but consider it this way. Perhaps as a young child the adult child began to learn the relationship between cause and effect in observing other people. The survival of the child is often dependent upon the child being able to anticipate adults' moods or behaviors and particularly in different situations. Consequently, one reason that all adult children of alcoholics have not been affected the same may be that the differences in personality and behaviors found in alcoholic parents are neither the same nor consistent.

Section Four

Different Reactions to Stress

Families under stress produce children under stress, but not all children react to stress the same way. Some adult children learned during their childhood to handle stress well and can still handle it. Other adult children have difficulty coping when put into stressful situations today, and much of their current stress reminds them of their childhood.

Although it is true that stress may produce many negative characteristics in children, it also is true that children may be able to develop prosocial behaviors to handle stress, and thus they are not as negatively affected. It may be possible to learn just as much from adult children who have developed high levels of resilience to stress as from adult children who break down under stress. By examining stress in childhood, it is possible to study how children in dysfunctional families learn to cope and adapt. How the adult child learned as a child to handle the stress of the alcoholic family may reveal clues as to how they handle stress today.

Again, it is obvious that adult children are affected differently by how they reacted differently to family stress.

According to Avis Brenner, the characteristics of children under stress in general, who are vulnerable to the negative aspects of stress, develop characteristics such as: (Brenner, 1984)

1. Overly sensitive and shy
2. Moody, irritable

3. Lonely, not able to make friends easily
4. Easily angered
5. Constantly complaining

Children who are extremely vulnerable to stress display these characteristics:

1. Withdrawn and preoccupied
2. Frequently sick without organic cause
3. Secretive, non-communicative
4. Belligerent
5. Prone to frequent nightmares

Obviously, not all children who are affected negatively by stress will possess all of the characteristics, but the adult child may be able to look back and identify with some of these behaviors as his or her way of handling stress. Even if you identified with some of these, however, you may feel that you had other ways of handling stress and that these were not as negative. This may be due to the fact that you were able to develop prosocial or resilient types of behaviors to handle stress.

For example, James Anthony describes the characteristics of children who have high levels of invulnerability to stress (Anthony, 1984). These behaviors include:

1. Children who know how to attract and use the support of adults.
2. Children who actively try to master their own environment and have a sense of their own power; often they volunteer to help others.
3. Children who develop a high degree of autonomy early in life.
4. Children who get involved in various activities or projects and do well in most things they do.
5. Children who are socially at ease and who make others feel comfortable around them.

Like most survivors of stress you probably possess a combination of the above patterns adapting to stress. Your particular combination probably depends on which patterns of coping behaviors you developed to handle the situation. Patterns of coping have positive and negative outcomes which depend upon whether they were long or short-term patterns. Generally, the longer the pattern of coping, the higher the probability that it became negative. This is particular true for the adult child who has carried his or her negative adaptive patterns from childhood stress into adulthood without adjusting or abandoning the negative aspects of the patterns.

How can patterns of coping with stress have both positive and negative aspects? It depends on the coping behavior and the degree to which the behavior is used to handle stress.

Four common ways for children to handle stress are: denial, regression, withdrawal, and impulsive acting out.

Therapists working with clients reared in alcoholic homes often interpret "denial" as a barrier to treatment, but it may have enabled the child to survive the parental alcoholism. For the child in a crisis, however, denial actually may be functional. For example, the child may at times deny that the problem exists in order to alleviate the emotional pain or to take time out from thinking about the situation. All children in stress need an "emotional vacation" from the stress in order to survive. Denial is one way to create this "time out."

Additionally, denial may be a way for the child to try to maintain a balance in his/her life. These aspects of denial for the child in stress thus become a pattern to help to handle the stress. Obviously, the negative side of denial occurs when it is carried to the point that no intervention is allowed because no problem is acknowledged to exist.

Regression is used by many children in stress as an attempt to return to a more secure state. For many children, brief periods of regression may have resulted in their being comforted by adults around them, thus reinforcing the regressive behavior of the child. The negative side of this develops when the child becomes too demanding for attention and develops an unhealthy sense of dependence, thus regressing to a point where he or she cannot or will not care for himself or herself.

Withdrawal, the third way of handling stress, can be used by children in crisis as a way of physically or emotionally removing themselves from the situation and of focusing attention elsewhere. This may provide relief for the child, but can become complicated if the withdrawal leads to isolation and a lack of contact with support systems.

Finally, there are some children of alcoholics, as well as other children in crisis situations, who engage in inappropriate "acting out" behavior. Although this may seem inappropriate to others, it actually may be a way for stressful children to draw attention to themselves instead of considering the real problems causing the stress. If carried to extremes, this pattern of coping becomes self destructive.

There are many other ways in which children under stress develop coping patterns. Perhaps you engaged in some of the above behaviors, or had other patterns which you still have in adulthood. Some of these other patterns might be the using of humor, helping others, and anticipating stressful situations.

Research has shown that adults who have a healthy sense of humor are more capable of handling stress well. This also was found to be true in young children. Rather than cry, you may have used sarcasm, jokes and humor to alleviate the seriousness of stressful situations.

Many adult children have become exceptionally adept at helping others. Have you ever wondered where the helping professions would be today without adult children of alcoholics? Forgetting your own problems by helping others may be a positive way to handle stress, as long as you do not forget yourself in the process. Helping others can provide a healthy and much needed sense of purpose, satisfaction and self-esteem for many adults. It helps to provide a sense of being needed and of accomplishment.

Finally, many adult children may have handled stress better than others because they learned to anticipate potentially stressful situations. They were able to foresee and plan accordingly and thus may have been better able to prepare to protect themselves. Were you the kind of adult child who could almost predict when the house would be exceptionally disrupted? If so, you may have been better prepared to handle the stress than adult children who were continually caught un-prepared.

All of these different responses to stress produce different outcomes. Those who had the greatest repertoire for handling stress are probably those adults today who still handle stress well. The Peter Principle states that the greatest part of courage is having done the thing before (Peters, 1970). Although none of us likes negative situations, some of us can handle them better than others.

Additionally, not all adults consider all stresses to be nega-tive. It is commonly agreed in research that some adults func-tion better under an optimal degree of stress, whereas others have difficulty handling even minimal stresses in their lives. Certainly, living with an alcoholic parent was a major stress for adult children of alcoholics, and not only how this stress was handled, but also the many different responses created, help to explain why adult children are not all affected the same way by having grown up as the child of an alcoholic.

Section Five

Perceptions of Growing Up in an Alcoholic Family

As an adult child of an alcoholic, your most critical variable is your perception of the situation while growing up. Families of alcoholics not only share different perceptions, but also individual family members will see different aspects of the same experience. Perceptions and reality are not always the same. Whatever you perceive as real, you probably react to accordingly. If you felt that you were in a totally hopeless situation while growing up, you probably reacted hopelessly. If you perceived that you had some control over the situation or that you were not alone, you may have perceived the situation as negative but not hopeless. Some adult children definitely feel that they were reared in extreme crisis situations, whereas others perceived that the crisis was manageable. Additionally, your perception not only of the situation but also of the degree to which you feel that you were affected emotionally must be considered. Table 3 illustrates the differences among adult children of alcoholics regarding their perceptions of the degree to which they feel they were emotionally affected by parental alcoholism.

As indicated on Table 3 the majority of adult children felt that they were highly affected, but almost one in four indicated that they were not. These different perceptions may have resulted from two considerations, the first being the degree of

TABLE 3

**Adult Children of Alcoholics' Perceptions of the Effects
of Parental Alcoholism on Their Lives**

Degree Affected	Percent of ACoA's (n=504)
Highly affected	78.2%
Moderately affected	11.1
Not affected	10.7

power you felt over the situation and the second, the degree to which you felt you had access to some help. What often makes a crisis a crisis is not just the situation itself, but whether or not the situation can be resolved or managed by you or others. Obviously, a crisis situation that is manageable is perceived as less detrimental than one over which you have no control.

Lee Ann Hoff in her book, *People in Crisis,* explains that a crisis develops in four phases (Hoff, 1984). In phase one the individual is exposed to a traumatic event and tries to use familiar problem-solving mechanisms to reduce or eliminate anxiety and concern. In phase two the individual's usual problem-solving abilities fail, thus anxiety and tension increase. Phase three begins when the person tries to use every available resource to solve the situation, but it remains unresolved and the anxiety increases further. This is especially true for the many families who isolate themselves because of alcoholism and thus unknowingly reduce the amount of available outside help. Phase four is when the person is in the crisis state. At this point internal strengths and social support are lacking, the problems remain unresolved, and the tension and anxiety reach an unbearable degree.

Adult children obviously were raised not only in a crisis situation, but also in a crisis of exceptional duration. Unlike the individual who experiences a short term traumatic event, the adult child was continually exposed. During this time the adult child began to perceive not only the situation, but also how he or she should react to the situation. I do not think that adult children of alcoholics planned their reactions, but rather did what seemed to make the most sense at the time. Besides, they may have perceived that they had little choice. Many of the different patterns of reactions by adult children may have been based on the degree of power that the adult child felt was available to control the situation. For most children of alcoholics, however, the sense of powerlessness over the situation further complicated having an alcoholic parent.

While growing up, the adult child was powerless over at least three problems.

1. The adult child was powerless to stop the alcoholic from drinking.

2. The adult child was powerless over the relationship between the parents as spouses. We know from research that the negative relationship between the parents is considered more detrimental than the drinking by the majority of children of alcoholics.

3. The adult child was powerless to leave while growing up. Many adult children initially saw their solution to the crisis as just a matter of leaving, only to find that while they may have physically removed themselves from the source of the crisis, many of the emotional issues remained unresolved. The initial idea was "All I have to do is leave and I will not only leave all of this behind, but also my life will automatically improve." However, many adult children left and discovered then that they did not have the psychological understanding to improve their lives.

Much of this stems from the outcomes possible from a crisis, which again explains why not all adult children are affected the same. Hoff states that three outcomes can happen to a person from a crisis (Hoff, 1984).

1. The person reduces the intolerable tension and anxiety by developing patterns of negative behaviors. These may range from becoming isolated, withdrawn or depressed to exaggerating the impact and blaming others for misfortune, or turning to self-destructive behaviors ranging from addiction to suicide.

2. The individual can return to a pre-crisis state. This is possible by using one's internal strengths and social support

networks to manage the crisis effectively. However, this outcome does not imply that new emotional growth has resulted from the experience, but instead the person has returned to his or her usual state of mind.

3. The person not only finds the problem manageable personally or with the help of others, but also the person grows from the experience and now uses the new problem solving skills for greater personal strength. It is possible that adult children may be found in all three of the categories, depending on their perceptions and their reactions to the perceptions in different patterns.

The problems of inconsistency in the alcoholic family, however, further complicate perception. For many adult children it was difficult to get an adequate and consistent perception of what was happening in their family. It is one thing to experience a crisis, and yet another to be in one that is highly inconsistent.

Judy Seixas and Geraldine Youcha refer to the alcoholic family as the "disorderly-orderly" family (Seixas, 1985). On one hand, the adult child remembers living in chaos and on the other, remembers trying to convince himself or herself that it was manageable or an "orderly" chaos. It is difficult to get an accurate perception of a situation which is characterized by mixed messages. The adult child may remember such statements as, "I love you; go away and leave me alone" or "There is nothing wrong, but don't tell anyone" or "I'm fine; call them up and tell them I am sick." These mixed messages contribute to the difficulty of developing an accurate perception. Some children of alcoholics, however, were able to develop perceptions of the situation that were not detrimental to them later as an adult child.

Those who developed less problematic perceptions may have been able to perceive that they were separate from the alcoholism, that they had power over themselves, that others were willing to help with the situation, or that their perceptions and the reality were synonymous. This enabled them to adjust more consistently and appropriately to parental alcoholism.

Section Six

Sons and Daughters of Alcoholics: Does Gender Make a Difference?

Are adult children of alcoholic mothers affected differently than adult children of alcoholic fathers? Do daughters of alcoholic mothers perceive the impact of parental alcoholism the same as sons? Do sons of alcoholic fathers experience the same emotional implications as daughters? What about the perceptions of sons and daughters of two alcoholic parents? It is obvious that there are many possible gender combinations that need to be considered when assessing why adult children are not all affected the same way.

To date, there has been little research on possible gender implications and differences of effects. Initially, there are several issues that need to be considered. One issue is related to how each gender fulfills his or her role as parent. Another is how each gender fulfills his or her role as an alcoholic parent. Are women or men more affected by alcoholism when it comes to being an effective parent? This side of the issue addresses the gender of the parent, but what about the gender of the adult child? It is possible that many of the generalizations about personality characteristics do not apply if the gender of the adult child is considered. Daughters of alcoholics may be affected differently than sons.

The tables in this section contain charts of the most commonly agreed upon personality characteristics found in adult children of alcoholics. These tables are concerned with the gender of the alcoholic and the gender of the adult child. The findings in these tables indicate that there are many similarities between sons and daughters of alcoholics, but differences of degree and areas affected are indicated. Additionally, it appears that the gender of the alcoholic parent or that having two alcoholic parents has different implications for sons and daughters.

Initially, however, it is helpful to compare the responses of adult children of alcoholics with those of adult sons and daughters of non-alcoholic parents. In Table 4 these comparisons are made. Sons and daughters of non-alcoholic parents scored almost identically, and there was almost an even split between which gender was more likely to identify with which characteristic. In fact, on four of the characteristics the scores were even, men scored higher on six items, and women scored higher on ten items. Additionally, the differences in scores on any individual item were small.

When comparing these scores to adult children of alcoholics, however, obvious differences become apparent. Besides the obvious difference that adult children scored higher than the control group, the differences between sons and daughters start to develop. For example, daughters of alcoholics had higher total scores on identifying with the personality characteristics. Additionally, the evenness between the two genders (half identifying with some characteristics and half identifying with others) begins to disappear. When parental alcoholism is considered, daughters now have higher scores on nineteen of the twenty items. Thus Table 4 not only reflects the similarity and differences between adults with alcoholic parents and those without, but for adult children of alcoholics it also raises the question of what accounts for these differences and under what parental gender differences are they most likely to increase or decrease?

TABLE 4

Personality Characteristics of Adult Sons and Daughters of Alcoholic and Non-Alcoholic Parents by Gender

	(Alcoholic Par)		(Non-Alcoholic)	
	Daughters	Sons	Daughters	Sons
1. I guess at what is normal.	3.19	3.04	2.51	2.51
2. I have difficulty following projects through to completion.	2.86	2.65	2.41	2.43
3. I lie when it would be just as easy to tell the truth.	2.18	2.23	1.81	1.81
4. I judge myself without mercy.	3.60	3.37	2.96	2.81
5. I have difficulty having fun.	3.13	3.06	2.37	2.50
6. I take myself very seriously.	3.92	3.65	3.40	3.40
7. I have difficulty with intimate relationships.	3.54	3.36	2.74	2.72
8. I overreact to changes over which I have no control.	3.42	3.16	2.83	2.73
9. I feel different from other people.	3.24	3.16	2.76	2.71
10. I constantly seek approval and affirmation.	3.48	3.37	3.01	2.96
11. I am either super responsible or irresponsible.	3.42	3.40	2.74	2.60
12. I am extremely loyal even in the face of evidence that the loyalty is undeserved.	3.41	3.21	3.04	3.03
13. I look for immediate as opposed to deferred gratification.	3.09	3.07	2.67	2.70
14. I lock myself into a course of action without serious consideration to alternate choices or consequences.	2.79	2.67	2.32	2.67
15. I seek tension and crisis and then complain.	2.65	2.40	2.12	2.05
16. I avoid conflict or aggravate it; but rarely deal with it.	2.83	2.77	2.42	2.42
17. I fear rejection and abandonment, yet I reject others.	3.11	2.85	2.35	2.38
18. I fear failure, but have difficulty handling success.	3.42	3.31	2.77	2.75
19. I fear criticism and judgment, yet I criticize others.	3.19	3.07	2.68	2.66
20. I manage my time poorly and do not set my priorities in a way that works well for me.	2.90	2.74	2.54	2.74
TOTALS	63.37	60.54	52.45	52.07

Score   5 = Always,   4 = Often,   3 = Sometimes,   2 = Seldom,   1 = Never

Alcoholic Mothers

Of the adult children of alcoholics in the national study, approximately 20% had an alcoholic mother. Although it is true that we do not know how many women alcoholics there are in our society, it does not appear that there are as many as male alcoholics. Although adult children of alcoholics may feel unique or different from others, those with alcoholic mothers may feel even more isolated because of several factors.

1. Having an alcoholic mother is not as common as having an alcoholic father.

2. Only one out of ten males will stay with an alcoholic female, compared with the nine out of ten women who will stay with an alcoholic male, thus greatly increasing the probability of single parenting for alcoholic women who are able to maintain child custody.

3. Societal implications for alcoholism in females may be different than for males because of greater stigmatization and the "fallen angel" syndrome of blaming the victim more in the case of women alcoholics.

4. There is the issue of the impact on children and child development when the mother is the alcoholic as opposed to the father. These considerations may make the adult child of an alcoholic mother consider himself or herself even more unique than adult children in general. However, we must not only consider the gender of the parent, but also the gender of the child.

Table 5 contains the differences in scores on personality characteristics of sons and daughters of alcoholic mothers. Thus the question is: Are sons and daughters affected in the same areas and to the same degrees, or is the effect of having an alcoholic mother different for daughters than for sons?

It appears in Table 5 that sons of alcoholic mothers have a greater degree of the personality characteristic identified with adult children of alcoholics. Although there are many similarities in scores between sons and daughters in Table 5, there are

TABLE 5

Personality Characteristics of Adult Sons and Daughters of Alcoholic Mothers

	Daughters	Sons
1. I guess at what is normal.	3.28	3.10
2. I have difficulty following projects through to completion.	2.84	2.50
3. I lie when it would be just as easy to tell the truth.	2.03	2.40
4. I judge myself without mercy.	3.42	3.25
5. I have difficulty having fun.	3.10	3.25
6. I take myself very seriously.	3.97	3.65
7. I have difficulty with intimate relationships.	3.45	3.75
8. I overreact to changes over which I have no control.	3.55	3.25
9. I feel different from other people.	3.27	3.30
10. I constantly seek approval and affirmation.	3.39	3.90
11. I am either super responsible or irresponsible.	3.42	3.85
12. I am extremely loyal even in the face of evidence that the loyalty is undeserved.	3.71	3.30
13. I look for immediate as opposed to deferred gratification.	3.00	3.30
14. I lock myself into a course of action without serious consideration to alternate choices or consequences.	2.74	2.60
15. I seek tension and crisis and then complain.	2.50	2.45
16. I avoid conflict or aggravate it, but rarely deal with it.	2.67	3.25
17. I fear rejection and abandonment, yet I reject others.	2.68	3.20
18. I fear failure, but have difficulty handling success.	3.13	3.35
19. I fear criticism and judgment, yet I criticize others.	2.87	3.50
20. I manage my time poorly and do not set my priorities in a way that works well for me.	2.74	2.60
TOTALS	61.76	63.75

Score   5 = Always,   4 = Often,   3 = Sometimes,   2 = Seldom,   1 = Never

some interesting differences. For example, the top three scores for daughters of alcoholic mothers were in the following areas:

Taking yourself very seriously

Being extremely loyal, and

Overreacting to change.

However, sons of alcoholic mothers rated three different issues as their top characteristics. These were:

Constantly seeking affirmation and approval

Being either super responsible or irresponsible,and
Having difficulty with intimate relationships.

Additionally, it is interesting to note the three areas where sons and daughters differ the most on their scores on personality characteristics. These differences were most notable in the areas of:

Fear of criticism and judgment
Seeking approval and affirmation,and
Avoiding conflict or aggravating it, but rarely dealing with it.

Although the overall degree of differences are not great, sons and daughters appear to be affected not only in different areas, but also to different degrees when exposed to maternal alcoholism. Sons of alcoholic mothers scored higher than daughters on 11 of the 20 characteristics. It is probable, therefore, that adult sons of alcoholic mothers have different issues to resolve than do daughters of alcoholic mothers, and the degree of resolution needed also will differ.

Alcoholic Fathers

It is much more common to have an alcoholic father in our society than an alcoholic mother. In this study approximately 60% of the adult children had an alcoholic father only. This statistic is in agreement with other studies. Although it may be more common, does having an alcoholic father have the same degree of effect on adult children as having an alcoholic mother, and again, do sons and daughters interpret the experience similarly? Table 6 contains the scores on personality characteristics of sons and daughters of alcoholic fathers. Although the personality characteristics are similar for both sons and daughters, one of the major differences is the areas that concern each the most. For daughters of alcoholic fathers, the highest three personality characteristics were:

taking herself very seriously
judging herself without mercy, and
constantly seeking approval and affirmation.

TABLE 6

Personality Characteristics of Adult Sons and Daughters of Alcoholic Fathers

	Daughters	Sons
1. I guess at what is normal.	3.15	3.01
2. I have difficulty following projects through to completion.	2.87	2.64
3. I lie when it would be just as easy to tell the truth.	2.20	2.18
4. I judge myself without mercy.	3.59	3.36
5. I have difficulty having fun.	3.10	2.99
6. I take myself very seriously.	3.90	3.64
7. I have difficulty with intimate relationships.	3.50	3.28
8. I overreact to changes over which I have no control.	3.46	3.11
9. I feel different from other people.	3.24	3.07
10. I constantly seek approval and affirmation.	3.51	3.28
11. I am either super responsible or irresponsible.	3.36	3.28
12. I am extremely loyal even in the face of evidence that the loyalty is undeserved.	3.34	3.25
13. I look for immediate as opposed to deferred gratification.	3.16	3.01
14. I lock myself into a course of action without serious consideration to alternate choices or consequences.	2.76	2.64
15. I seek tension and crisis and then complain.	2.62	2.36
16. I avoid conflict or aggravate it but rarely deal with it.	2.85	2.66
17. I fear rejection and abandonment, yet I reject others.	3.22	2.75
18. I fear failure, but have difficulty handling success.	3.48	3.28
19. I fear criticism and judgment, yet I criticize others.	3.32	2.95
20. I manage my time poorly and do not set my priorities in a way that works well for me.	2.88	2.78
TOTALS	63.51	59.52

Score 5 = Always, 4 = Often, 3 = Sometimes, 2 = Seldom, 1 = Never

It is interesting to note that when the mother was alcoholic, adult sons and daughters had different areas of concerns. Sons of alcoholic fathers, on the other hand, had the same top three concerns as daughters of alcoholic fathers but to different degrees (items scores were carried to the .000 level to determine differences). Thus, for sons of alcoholic fathers the top three areas of concern were:

taking himself very seriously
judging himself without mercy, and
constantly seeking approval and affirmation.

The greatest differences for sons and daughters occurred in these areas:

> fear of rejection and abandonment
> fear of criticism and judgment, and
> overreacting to changes over which one has no control.

Again, as was the case with having an alcoholic mother, sons and daughters appear to be affected differently, but to a lesser degree of variation in the ranking of personality characteristics. What is strikingly different in the case of the alcoholic father is that daughters scored higher on all 20 personality characteristics than sons. This was not the case with the alcoholic mother, where the son scored higher on eleven of the characteristics. This finding does raise interesting speculation and implications for cross-gender alcoholism, in which the alcoholic is the opposite gender of the adult child. Both of these cases, however, have one thing in common for both sons and daughters, and that is that only one of the parents was alcoholic. What about the effects on sons and daughters who grew up with two alcoholic parents?

Two Alcoholic Parents

In approximately 20% of the cases in this study, adult children of alcoholics had two alcoholic parents. Research indicates that where both parents are alcoholic the alcoholism developed at earlier ages for both parents, thus increasing the probability that children of alcoholics are exposed to parental alcoholism at earlier ages themselves than when only one parent is alcoholic. Additionally, other research suggests that adult children of two alcoholic parents are more likely to begin drinking themselves at earlier ages and that they are themselves more susceptible to alcoholism at earlier ages. Where both parents are alcoholic, there may be a variety of other associated issues that compound parental alcoholism for children. For example, there is not the presence of the non-alcoholic spouse to fill in as parent as an offsetting factor. Or the children may be faced with more emotional and physical neglect, which may lead to a higher probability of foster placement than in families with one alcoholic parent. Table 7 contains the responses of sons and daughters of two alcoholic parents.

Table 7 shows that daughters of two alcoholic parents appear to be more affected than sons. Both sons and daughters share two out of three of their top areas of concerns, but again the degree of impact is different. For daughters of two alcoholic parents, their top three characteristics were:

> Taking herself very seriously
> Judging herself without mercy, and
> Having difficulty with intimate relationships.

Sons of two alcoholic parents ranked the following characteristics the highest:

> Taking himself very seriously
> Having difficulty with intimate relationships, and
> Being super responsbile or irresponsible

The greatest differences in scores of characteristics between sons and daughters of two alcoholic parents occurred in the areas of:

> Being extremely loyal
> Taking themselves very seriously, and
> Judging themselves without mercy

Over all the variable of gender appears to have a significant impact on the issues that are identified for sons and daughters of alcoholics. It is difficult, however, to distinguish the exact relationship of gender implications. That is, is it the gender of the parent that makes a difference, the gender of the adult child, or a combination of the interaction of both genders? Additionally, one could consider another side of the gender issue which examines the master status roles that parents play in their childrens' lives.

For example, is it more critical to impair the performance of one of the parental roles than the other? Another factor might be the effect on how the child fulfills his or her own role when one of the parental roles is impaired. If the mother is alcoholic,

TABLE 7

Characteristics of Adult Sons and Daughters of Two Alcoholic Parents

	Daughters	Sons
1. I guess at what is normal.	3.27	3.07
2. I have difficulty following projects through to completion.	2.86	2.69
3. I lie when it would be just as easy to tell the truth.	2.20	2.31
4. I judge myself without mercy.	3.74	3.44
5. I have difficulty having fun.	3.21	3.16
6. I take myself very seriously.	3.96	3.64
7. I have difficulty with intimate relationships.	3.72	3.51
8. I overreact to changes over which I have no control.	3.32	3.24
9. I feel different from other people.	3.22	3.36
10. I constantly seek approval and affirmation.	3.48	3.38
11. I am either super responsible or irresponsible.	3.56	3.50
12. I am extremely loyal even in the face of evidence that the loyalty is undeserved.	3.49	3.00
13. I look for immediate as opposed to deferred gratification.	3.00	3.09
14. I lock myself into a course of action without serious consideration to alternate choices or consequences.	2.90	2.80
15. I seek tension and crisis and then complain.	2.80	2.53
16. I avoid conflict or aggravate it; but rarely deal with it.	2.85	2.93
17. I fear rejection and abandonment, yet I reject others.	3.09	3.02
18. I fear failure, but have difficulty handling success.	3.43	3.33
19. I fear criticism and judgment, yet I criticize others.	3.01	3.24
20. I manage my time poorly and do not set my priorities in a way that works well for me.	2.96	2.76
TOTALS	64.07	62.00

Score 5 = Always, 4 = Often, 3 = Sometimes, 2 = Seldom, 1 = Never

this obviously affects her performance as a parent, but how does her role impairment affect or cause changes in the child's role? Are children of alcoholics more capable of adjusting and handling the impairment of one parental role better than the other?

Another gender consideration is: How does the alcoholism in one parent affect the ability of the other parent to fulfill his or her parental responsiblities? For example, the first variable discussed in this booklet asked how the degree of alcoholism in the alcoholic parent affects the ability of the parent to fulfill his or her role as parent. However, what about how well the non-alcoholic parent fulfills his or her role? This may be a gender issue as well. If the mother is alcoholic, this obviously affects her role, but how does it also affect the ability of her husband to be an effective parent?

In a study by Carol Williams this issue was considered (Williams, 1983). She studied approximately 100 families and was concerned with the effects on the quality of child care, depending on which parent was the alcoholic. Williams examined the gender of the alcoholic parent and effects on children by examining the quality of child care, the level of family stability, incidence of any child abuse, and child neglect. Table 8 illustrates her findings. In the table all rankings are shown as high, middle or low to illustrate the differences in rank between the effects of an alcoholic father only, an alcoholic mother only, or two alcoholic parents.

This study demonstrates again the different influences that gender of alcoholic parent can have on children. It also raises some interesting issues. In the above case of two alcoholic parents, we see that the quality of child care was the lowest and that the level of child abuse was the highest. This would agree with other research that indicates that if both parents are alcoholic, the alcoholism was likely to develop at earlier ages and that younger parents are more likely to abuse children physically than are older parents (Straus, 1980). The findings on alcoholic mothers only show that this causes the least family stability. However, we know that very few husbands will stay with an alcoholic wife and thus contribute to this problem by leaving. For fathers only, however, many of the issues appear not to be as devastating.

This effect was also found among the adult children, as indicated on the earlier tables, where having an alcoholic father only produced lower scores by the adult children on the personality items. Is this due to the fact that alcoholism in fathers is not as critical for children or is it due to other

TABLE 8

Gender of Alcoholic Parent and the Quality of Child Care

	Quality of Child Care	Family Stability	Child Abuse	Neglect
Both Parents	low	middle	high	middle
Mother Only	middle	low	middle	high
Father Only	high	high	low	low

factors? Again, the answer may be that it is a gender issue, particularly because we are concerned with the quality of child care and we know that in the cases of male alcoholism the majority of women will stay. Thus it may be that she is directly or indirectly fulfilling many of the parenting responsibilities and reducing the impact of his drinking in certain areas for the children. An interesting question to consider might be: Is it possible that women can tolerate alcoholism better in their spouses and still fulfill their roles as parents than men can tolerate alcoholism in their spouses and still fulfill their roles as parents? The issue of gender is a highly interactive variable with a diversity of outcomes for adult children of alcoholics.

From this discussion and presentation of the national data, what gender combinations then are the most devastating for adult daughters and adult sons?

Using the total scores on the different personality character-istics, it appears that for daughters of alcoholics, having two alcoholic parents has the greatest impact, followed by having an alcoholic father, and least by having an alcoholic mother. For sons of alcoholic parents, the greatest impact occurred when he had an alcoholic mother. Next was having two alco-holic parents, and the least impact on sons was that of having an alcoholic father.

It is interesting to note that both adult sons and daughters scored lowest on the personality characteristics when their alcoholic parent was of the same gender. It should be noted, however, that the range of scores for each of the gender com-binations was not that great, but the degree and the differences in which personality characteristics were most identified were important. Thus, for example, daughters of alcoholic mothers may have diffferent issues to work on in recovery than if they had an alcoholic father or both parents alcoholic. Sons of alcoholics also have different issues that they will bring to recovery. Additionally, it is obvious that both sons and daughters of alcoholic parents of either gender will have much in common and that the powerful issues of self criticism, taking yourself too seriously, needing approval, being extremely loyal and, most important, having difficulty with intimate relationships will dominate the recovery process.

Section Seven

Does Age Make a Difference?

Age can affect the outcome of exposure to parental alcoholism in a variety of ways. One is how old the child was when parental alcoholism developed. If you were born into an alcoholic home, conditions may be very different than if your parent became alcoholic when you were five or fifteen. Thus it is not only the exposure to alcoholism that is significant, but also when the exposure for the adult child began.

Additionally, it is doubtful that the child was aware of alcoholism as the problem in his or her home, but rather realized that he or she lived in a house that was "different". Being exposed to alcoholism and understanding alcoholism may be two different things, the understanding of both of which may be related to age. A young child may be able to understand the physical effects of getting drunk long before he or she can understand the dynamics of alcoholism and its impact on the family, particularly on family relationships. Age becomes an important factor when we consider the adult child from a developmental perspective. That is, what is the effect of parental alcoholism on children at different ages?

Additionally, a developmental approach would consider what the normal developmental issues are for the child at that age and how these normal problems are compounded by exposure to parental alcoholism. According to Erikson and his developmental levels, some of the normal issues to be resolved by young children focus on the development of trust, of a sense of autonomy, of initiative, and of a sense of accomplishment (Erickson, 1963). Besides working through these normal childhood issues, the young child of the alcoholic will face the additional ones arising from having an alcoholic parent.

For example, if your parent became alcoholic when you were eight, you were far more likely to be concerned with your physical safety, with fear of abandonment, and with parental arguments than you were with the drinking.

In her work with young children of alcoholics, Ellen Morehouse identifies seven major areas of concerns that affect children at this age who have an alcoholic parent (Morehouse, 1982). These concerns are:

1. Worrying about the health of the alcoholic parent.
2. Being upset and angry by the unpredictable and inconsistent behavior of the alcoholic parent and the lack of support from the non-alcoholic parent.
3. Worrying about fights and arguments between their parents.
4. Being scared and upset by the violence or the possibility of violence in their family.
5. Being upset by the parent's inappropriate behavior, which can include criminal or sexual behavior.
6. Being disappointed by broken promises and by feeling unloved.
7. Feeling responsible for their parent's drinking.

If these are for children, why mention them for adult children of alcoholics? How many of these feelings do you still have now, or how did exposure to these issues affect your childhood? How has your childhood affected your adulthood? Adult children who were not exposed to parental alcoholism during their early childhood may have different perceptions of the experience, as well as of their childhood. How you handled these issues then may affect you now.

What about your adolescence and parental alcoholism? This developmental age is argued by many to be the most critical because it is concerned not only with identity formation, but also with issues of sexuality and the development of the ability to achieve positive emotional intimacy in our lives. By the time some people become adolescents, they already will have experienced parental alcoholism because it started during their childhood, whereas for others the alcoholism developed during their adolescence.

The major areas of concern for adolescent children of alcoholics are (Ackerman, 1986):

1. Concerned about their own substance use and if alcoholism is hereditary.
2. Concerned about the health of or how to get their alcoholic parent to stop drinking.
3. How to survive their parents' troubled relationship.
4. Concerned about their family's alcoholism and its effects on their friendships, dating, and "reputation."
5. How to live with an alcoholic.
6. How to develop better survival skills for coping and getting help.
7. Concerned about other issues that may be related, such as physical abuse, incest, or how and why they may be affected by alcoholism.

If you are an adult child, which of these concerns remain with you today? Although you may have experienced exposure to parental alcoholism years ago, your age at the time of exposure still may have a profound effect on you today. During your adolescence you were confronted with the normal issues of establishing your identity, formulating your sexuality, and preparing yourself for achieving intimacy at the same time. As a child of an alcoholic, however, you may have had the additional issues mentioned above impacting on you. Many unresolved issues in adolescence are carried over into adulthood, and the adult child may find himself or herself unable to confront these issues and thereby be trapped in "perpetual adolescence" in certain areas of their lives.

Another factor is not only at what age you first were exposed, but also how old you were when you were willing to acknowledge that one or both of your parents had a drinking problem. In the national study it was interesting to note that not only did adult children acknowledge the status of an alcoholic parent at different ages, but also the gender of the alcoholic parent influenced when they acknowledged it. Table 9 contains the different ages of adult children when they first acknowledged that one or both parents had a drinking problem.

TABLE 9

Age of Adult Children of Alcoholics When Parental Alcoholism was Acknowledged

Alcoholic Parent	Average Age
Both Parents	14.3 years
Father only	12.7
Mother only	18.4

As indicated in Table 9, the ages of acknowledgment differed depending upon the gender of the alcoholic. Between alcoholic mothers and alcoholic fathers, there appears to be a notable difference in the age at which acknowlegment by the adult child occurred. It is obvious that this situation is more than just an age factor and that it is closely related to the previous discussions of gender implications.

The later recognition for alcoholism in mothers may be caused by several factors. One research indicates that women develop alcoholism later in life than men, therefore their ages and the ages of their children would be higher. Second, having an alcoholic mother as opposed to an alcoholic father may be harder for some children to accept. Finally, alcoholism in women is not as readily accepted in society as in men, and therefore the denial process may be even longer in the case of maternal alcoholism. This elongated denial of maternal alcoholism may account for the average age at which adult children of two alcoholic parents acknowledged the condition. It would seem that having two alcoholic parents would be acknowledged more quickly than having one. However, the delay in accepting maternal alcoholism appears to increase the average age in the case of two alcoholic parents.

Another factor to consider in the case of two alcoholic parents is that the alcoholism may not have developed at the same time in both parents.

The last issues about age and the diversity of effects on adult children of alcoholics are concerned with how old you are now. These age considerations raise two issues. One is what the normal developmental issues are that all people your age normally experience. Two, are the problems for adult children of alcoholism more likely to become apparent at particular ages, and if so, at what age?

Initially, the adult child must be able to separate what are normal developmental issues of adulthood such as intimacy, generativity (which is the ability to give beyond yourself to the next generation), a sense of integrity, and the ability to self-actualize. These issues are difficult in themselves for all adults, let alone for adult children of alcoholics who will experience these as well as a variety of other issues related to parental alcoholism.

Thus adult children will bring their own set of unique age issues related to parental alcoholism not unlike those of young children and adolescents of alcoholics. It is important to recognize at this point, however, that the adult child will have a combination of normal developmental concerns and the unique problems of being an adult child of an alcoholic. These two areas combine to impede, arrest or accelerate the human developmental process. Additionally, some of these will be carried over from childhood or adolescence, and others will develop in adulthood.

At what age in adulthood are they most likely to manifest themselves? Table 10 compares the personality characteristic scores of adult children of alcoholics with adults of non-alcoholic parents at different ages. Not only does this table indicate at what ages the characteristics are most noticeable, but also at what ages the differences between adult children and adults in general are the greatest.

As indicated in Table 10 adult children of alcoholics are

TABLE 10

Differences in Personality Characteristics by Age in Adult Children of Alcoholics and Adults of Non-Alcoholic Parents

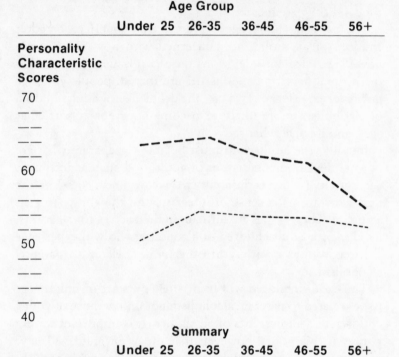

	Age Group				
	Under 25	26-35	36-45	46-55	56+

Personality Characteristic Scores

Summary

	Under 25	26-35	36-45	46-55	56+
ACA	63.15	63.90	60.92	59.47	53.96
Non ACA	50.59	54.15	52.74	53.16	52.57
% Difference	24.82%	18.05%	15.51%	11.86%	2.64%

Key: ACA — — —   Non ACA ----

most affected until their mid-thirties, at which time the degree to which they are affected begins to decline. Additionally, it is during these years that the greatest differences between adult children and adults of non-alcoholic parents are apparent. These years, however, for most adults are highly transitional ones regarding careers, families and relationships, but for adult children of alcoholics the normal stresses of these years may accentuate the many personality characteristics from difficult childhoods. Thus the stresses of childhood may be particularly noticeable during the stresses of adulthood. It is interesting to note that as both groups mature and some of the transitional stress is eliminated, the differences begin to disappear until finally the two groups merge.

The age factor is related to the concept of "recovery lag," in which not all parts of the individual will need the same degree of intervention, nor will all parts of the individual recover at the same rate. It is possible that the adult child will need to work on different issues that occurred at different ages in his or her life, particularly if these issues have remained largely unresolved. Thus the adult child, although an adult, finds himself or herself emotionally affected by experiences that occurred at different ages of his or her life. A positive side of this for adult children, however, is that at this point they may now possess more emotional support and interpersonal skills for resolving issues than they possessed when they were younger. Thus the motto of "survive now and heal later" may make sense, since now the adult may have more resources for understanding and resolving issues that he or she was not previously capable of handling.

Although childhood may severely affect adulthood for adult children, the adult child must remember that he or she now can act to reduce the detrimental impact of his or her experiences of childhood. As a young child of an alcoholic, your age may have worked against you and kept you from being able to seek help or resolve issues, but as an adult you now can use your age as an asset to release any negative childhood experiences. Again, this task will be a process with many factors influencing the outcome, but certainly age is one of the main factors. The longer your exposure to active alcoholism, the higher the probability that it will have produced more issues for you to resolve. An adult child whose parent became alcoholic when the child was ten and then achieved sobriety when the child was twenty-two, may have very different feelings than an adult child who was born into an alcoholic home and whose parent is still drinking.

Additionally, for the few fortunate adult children whose parent has quit drinking, age still may be a factor. For example, how old were you when the parent became sober? In the national study the average age of adult children whose parent became sober was 24.3 years. These adult children may have entirely different perceptions, issues, and attitudes about parental alcoholism than adult children whose parents have never stopped drinking, thus the adult child never has had the opportunity to know the alcoholic parent sober.

Section Eight

Offsetting Contributing Factors

Not all variations of effects on adult children of alcoholics can be understood easily. Many differences in effects may be due to unknown or "offsetting factors" in the adult child's life. These offsetting factors may be other people or institutions that have had a positive effect on the adult child either now or when the adult was growing up. What these individuals or institutions accomplished, either knowingly or unknowingly, was that they were able to provide the adult child with positive role models, emotional support, meaningful activities, a sense of belonging, or simply a much needed diversion from the family conflict.

It is difficult to assess the impact of offsetting factors, but for the adult child it is important to realize the positive impact that they may have had on the adult child's life. The importance of the offsetting person or institution may be that it was able to help provide a "balance" in the adult child's life. For example, school may have been an offsetting factor for some adult children because it provided not only a physical break from family involvement, but also an emotional recess from thinking about the family. Additionally, for those adult children who did well in school or felt that they belonged socially, the school experience may have been able to provide a positive self-concept that was not offered in the home.

Another aspect of offsetting factors involves the importance of primary relationships in one's life. For adult children of alcoholics who remember having close and primary relationships outside of the family, the impact of the alcoholism may have been reduced, since they had an identity that was separate from the alcoholism.

For adult children who were withdrawn and physically or emotionally isolated, however, the impact of the parental alcoholism may have been felt even more severely. An adult child who had friends and belonged to several organizations or groups, had the opportunity to have meaningful interactions during his or her day. The "loner" child, however, only increased the degree of isolation already felt by most children of alcoholics because of lack of outside support systems.

Besides belonging to institutions or groups, adult children may have had a particular person who was a significant individual in his or her life and who helped reduce the impact of parental alcoholism. This may have been a sibling, relative, best friend, or an adult who interacted positively with the adult child. It is possible that this could have been the non-alcoholic parent as well. In a study on adult children of alcoholics in Poland it was found that among adult children who were now doing well as opposed to those who were not, the intervening variable that made a difference was that the adult children doing well all had a very positive image of how their non-alcoholic parent fulfilled his or her role as parent (Obuchowska, 1974). Thus the non-alcoholic parent's ability to fulfill the parental role successfully served as a significant offsetting factor for the alcoholic parent's impact.

In Table 11 the percent of adult children who stated that they were able to share their feelings with someone about the parental alcoholism is indicated.

TABLE 11

Percent of Adult Children of Alcoholics Who Received Help With Their Feelings

Received help	10.8%
Did not receive help	89.2%

Unfortunately, as indicated on Table 11, the vast majority of adult children did not receive help with their feelings from anyone while they were growing up. This does not mean, however, that offsetting factors did not occur. As stated earlier, help could have been directly or indirectly received.

For the adult child, what kinds of activities or persons can be identified as "contributing others" in their lives? What benefits did they derive from interaction with others who helped them maintain an emotional balance? This may have been accomplished in the adult child's life even though those with whom he or she interacted did not know the "family secret". On the other hand, there may have been those with whom you could share the family secret and from whom you could derive support, even though the situation was not resolved. It is important, therefore, for the adult child to realize that the offsetting factors were indeed positive and that establishing them and maintaining them now may continue to serve the adult child with a positive sense of identity, support, and acceptance.

Section Nine

Cultural Considerations

All of us possess individual and family differences, some genetically inherited and others socially acquired. These differences include our race, ethnicity, religions, values, and family norms. It is important to take these variables into consideration because the adult child (like all children) was raised in his or her own particular social context. Thus a Black adult child may have similar experiences to Hispanic or White adult children, but at the same time may have different experiences related to alcoholism in the Black community which the others did not experience. The same is true for the other groups. Again, the experience of parental alcoholism may be common, but how each family's system of values, race, ethnic composition, and religion respond may indicate the need for appreciation of cultural considerations.

For example, is it different to be a child of an alcoholic in a family where the religion forbids the use of any alcohol, as opposed to being in an alcoholic family that does not? Does alcoholism affect the minority family more, less, or differently than it does majority families? In most societies, the further you are away from the average or the norm in the society, the more other societal issues will impact on you and your family. If you represent the average in your society, however, most of the societal norms and practices represent your orientation. Thus the majority adult child may not have the "extra issues" to accompany his or her status that a minority adult child may bring into focus. The minority adult child may have many of the same feelings and can identify with the issues affecting all adult children, but he or she also may have his or her additional considerations of being a minority.

Alcoholism does not affect all groups the same. There are differences in rates of prevalence, gender, recovery, and utilization of human services for intervention.

Table 12 indicates the differences in scores of adult children by race in the United States. Additionally, Table 12 indicates the differences among each race between adults with alcoholic parents and those with non-alcoholic parents.

These differences are apparent in the scores of adults with non-alcoholic parents, in which Blacks possessed the personality characteristics the least and Native Americans identified with them the most. When parental alcoholism was considered, this pattern remained the same. It was interesting to note the percentages of increases in scores for each race, however; Hispanics with alcoholic parents had the greatest increase in personality characteristics, followed in order by Blacks, Whites, and Native Americans over adults with non-alcoholic parents. Additionally, even though Native Americans had the highest scores for the non-alcoholic group, they had the lowest increase in scores when parental alcoholism occurred. It is difficult to speculate as to the cause in differences in scores, but each group must be assessed for its uniqueness in order to fully understand the adult child in his or her social context.

TABLE 12

Differences in Personality Characteristics by Race in Adult Children of Alcoholics and Adults of Non-Alcoholic Parents

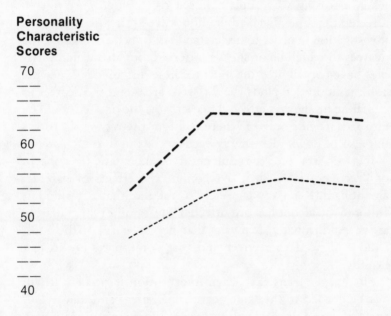

	Black	Hispanic	Native American	White

Personality Characteristic Scores

	Summary			
	Black	**Hispanic**	**Native American**	**White**
ACA	54.00	64.30	64.77	62.75
Non ACA	45.05	52.00	56.21	52.96
% Difference	19.9%	23.7%	15.2%	18.5%

Key: ACA — — — Non ACA ----

Summary

These eight variables are some of the major considerations when assessing why adult children of alcoholics are not all affected the same. Each adult child will require his or her own investigation in order to understand not only differences in the degrees to which he or she was affected, but also which variables have contributed the most to these differences. Once the adult child understands the different areas and the degrees to which he or she was affected in each area, he or she should be more aware not only of where to begin the recovery process but also of how much energy needs to be put into each area.

It is important for the adult child to understand the concept of "recovery lag" when overcoming the effects of parental alcoholism. Recovery lag refers to the fact that not all adult children of alcoholics are affected the same or in the same areas. Additionally, it means that not all parts of the adult child will need to recover and that some parts are in fact healthy.

Finally, it means that when intervention is needed, it will not be needed to the same degree in all areas and that not all parts of the adult child will recover at the same rate. Although all adult children share the common bond of having at least one alcoholic parent, it is important to understand that each adult child is unique, not only in the experiences that he or she has had but also in the degree to which these contribute to who the adult child is today. Then the adult can understand and accept the person he or she is today and become the person that he or she would like to be tomorrow.

Appendix

The data used in this booklet is from the National Adult Children of Alcoholics Research Study conducted at Indiana University of Pennsylvania under the Faculty Research Associate Program. The principal investigator is Robert J. Ackerman, Ph.D., Associate Professor of Sociology. This study is an exploratory descriptive study that was designed to assess the personality characteristics of adult children of alcoholics from adults of non-alcoholic parents and to develop an assessment instrument for future research on adult children of alcoholics.

The data utilized in this booklet were collected by survey research from approximately one thousand adults, of which approximately half had at least one alcoholic parent. This data was collected from thirty-eight states. Adult children of alcoholics were self-identified and may or may not have been in treatment (only 20% had ever gone to any treatment related to being an adult child of an alcoholic).

References

Ackerman, Robert J. "The National Adult Children of Alcoholics Research Study" Indiana University of Pennsylvania, Indiana, Pennsylvania, 1987.

Ackerman, Robert J. In **Growing in the Shadow**. Edited by Robert J. Ackerman, Health Communications, Pompano Beach, FL, 1986.

Anthony, James. In "Resilient Children" by Maya Pines, *American Educator*, Fall, 1984.

Brenner, Avis. **Helping Children Cope with Stress**. Lexington Books, Lexington, MA, 1984.

Erikson, E. H. **Childhood and Society**. W.W. Norton and Co., New York, NY, 1963.

Greenleaf, Jael. Presentation at the Regional Children of Alcoholics Conference, sponsored by The U.S. Journal of Drug and Alcohol Dependence, Los Angeles, CA, November, 1984.

Hoff, Lee Ann. **People in Crisis**. 2nd ed., Addison-Wesley Publishing, Menlo Park, CA, 1984.

Morehouse, Ellen and T. Richards. "An Examination of Dysfunctional Latency Age Children of Alcoholic Parents and Problems in Intervention". *Journal of Children in Contemporary Society*, 15 (1), 1982.

Obuchowska, I. "Emotional Contact with the Mother as a Social Compensatory Factor in Children of Alcoholics". *International Mental Health Research Newsletter*, 16 (4), 2:4, 1974.

Peter, Lawrence and Raymond Hull. **The Peter Principle**. Bantam Books, New York, NY, 1970.

Seixas, Judy and Geraldine Youcha. **Children of Alcoholism**. Crown Publishing, New York, NY, 1985.

Strauss, M., R. Gelles and S. Steinmetz. **Behind Closed Doors: Violence in the American Family**. Anchor Press, Garden City, NY, 1980.

Wegscheider-Cruse, Sharon and Don Wegscheider. **Family Illness: Chemical Dependency**. Nurturing Networks, Crystal, MN, 1978.

Williams, Carol N. "Differences in Child Care Practices Among Families with Alcoholic Fathers, Alcoholic Mothers, and Two Alcoholic Parents". Dissertation Abstracts International, 44 (01), 299-A, 1983.